YOU KNO[...]
MOBILE ADDI[...]

Emma B[...]

SUMMERSDALE

Copyright © Summersdale Publishers Ltd 2001

Summersdale Publishers Ltd
46 West Street
Chichester
PO19 1RP

www.summersdale.com

ISBN 1 84024 204 3

Printed and bound in Great Britain

Text by Emma Burgess
Cartoons by Kate Taylor

You know you're a mobile addict when...

YOU KNOW YOU'RE A MOBILE ADDICT WHEN . . .

In the throes of passion, you'd rather text your partner than express your love via the gift of speech.

YOU KNOW YOU'RE A MOBILE ADDICT WHEN . . .

Your facial expressions are slightly less expressive than emoticons.

YOU KNOW YOU'RE A MOBILE ADDICT WHEN . . .

Your mobile phone provider no longer sends you itemised bills... it costs them too much man-time (and trees) to print it out.

6

Local hospitals are aware of your hazardous effect. You even accept phone calls when on the operating table...having new ears grafted on.

8

YOU KNOW YOU'RE A MOBILE ADDICT WHEN . . .

Your parents haven't called you for over a year... they don't understand this mobile lark.

YOU KNOW YOU'RE A MOBILE ADDICT WHEN . . .

You were admitted to *The Priory* when you mislaid your phone for a day.

YOU KNOW YOU'RE A MOBILE ADDICT WHEN . . .

You'd rather ruin someone's wedding vows than miss a call.

Your friends tell you to
network more, so you host
a party for *Orange*,
Vodafone and *Cellnet*.

You won't visit your friends in the country... well, there's no reception out it the sticks.

15

Your idea of a romantic evening would be spent playing *Snake* or *Rotation* for two.

You have a wet-suit made
for your phone so you can
take it into the shower
with you.

17

You buy your dog a mobile
and encourage him to text
'woof' instead of barking.

YOU KNOW YOU'RE A MOBILE ADDICT WHEN . . .

People are impressed to hear that you are a composer. What they don't realise is that you compose mobile ring tones.

20

YOU KNOW YOU'RE A MOBILE ADDICT WHEN . . .

You design the first mobile phone for use in Outer Space... afterall, those poor astronauts have a life outside of the Space Shuttle.

You have been banned from flying after making a call on a trans-Atlantic flight...which sent the plane careering towards Jupiter instead.

Your mobile phone service
provider employs a huge
team of people to deal
with your account alone.

24

You have forgotten how to write. There's little point when texting is so efficient.

25

YOU KNOW YOU'RE A MOBILE ADDICT WHEN . . .

You can't recall what your friends look like because there's no need to see them now you have their numbers.

YOU KNOW YOU'RE A MOBILE ADDICT WHEN . . .

You turn down a free holiday to some exotic location, because your phone's roam facility has been disabled.

Don't speak to me... Just call.

You love to accessorise... your mobile phone must always match your shoes and handbag.

YOU KNOW YOU'RE A MOBILE ADDICT WHEN . . .

You take *hands-free* one step too far...your ear piercings are large enough to insert a mobile phone.

Don't speak to me... Just call.

YOU KNOW YOU'RE A MOBILE ADDICT WHEN . . .

You are saving up for
a headset implant.

YOU KNOW YOU'RE A MOBILE ADDICT WHEN . . .

You live in near darkness
and without television...
every socket in your
house is being used
by a phone charger.

You have a phone pouch incorporated into the design of your wedding dress...just in case you get a better offer over phone on the big day.

33

YOU KNOW YOU'RE A MOBILE ADDICT WHEN . . .

You petition for the demolition of all train tunnels because your phone doesn't work in them.

YOU KNOW YOU'RE A MOBILE ADDICT WHEN . . .

You can text message
faster than you can type.

YOU KNOW YOU'RE A MOBILE ADDICT WHEN . . .

You can't understand how your great-grandfather survived two World Wars without the use of a mobile.

YOU KNOW YOU'RE A MOBILE ADDICT WHEN . . .

The closest you've ever come to being incommunicado was switching your phone onto its silent mode.

Don't speak to me... Just call.

YOU KNOW YOU'RE A MOBILE ADDICT WHEN . . .

Scientists use you as their willing guinea pig for neurological research and discover that, since using your mobile more, your brain is actually half the size of a real guinea pig's.

Don't speak to me... Just call.

You brag about your
mobile home...
the caravan used to
store all your phones.

When your toddler nephew requests a mobile for Christmas, he's upset when you buy him a phone to hang above his cot.

40

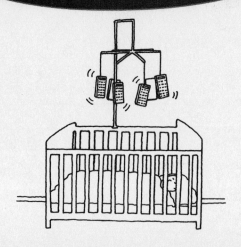

YOU KNOW YOU'RE A
MOBILE ADDICT WHEN . . .

YOU KNOW YOU'RE A MOBILE ADDICT WHEN . . .

You are arrested in Paris for defacing the Mona Lisa. You think she looks somehow better with the mobile phone you added in biro.

The first thing you do in the morning is shake the phones out of your bed.

YOU KNOW YOU'RE A MOBILE ADDICT WHEN . . .

Your friends are fed up with your inability to speak without your hand raised to your ear.

YOU KNOW YOU'RE A MOBILE ADDICT WHEN . . .

You look lopsided because your phone ear has been flattened from over-use.

You carry so many phones
with different ringing
tones that when someone
else's phone goes off you
always assume it's for you.

YOU KNOW YOU'RE A MOBILE ADDICT WHEN . . .

You think that combat trousers (with their myriad pockets for phones) are the greatest invention... since the mobile phone, obviously.

YOU KNOW YOU'RE A MOBILE ADDICT WHEN . . .

You develop such sensitive hearing that it enables you to listen intently on your mobile phone even when in the noisiest nightclub.

48

You pay millions to have bat-like sonic radars implanted into your ears. This way you can hear your phone even if you've left it at home (fat chance).

You dumped your lover by text, even though you live in the same house.

Other people save up for
their retirement homes
but you reserve your bed
in a tumour ward.

Your mother was
horrified at your birth to
discover a recharge lead
where the umbilical cord
should have been.

You write poetry in the vowel-less language of text and are awarded a prize for promoting creative writing in Welsh.

53

You are fired from your job helping aircraft taxi to the terminal building because you dropped one of your bats to take a call.

54

You can't see the point of
sports that require you to
leave your phone behind.

YOU KNOW YOU'RE A MOBILE ADDICT WHEN . . .

You give up scuba diving when you nearly drowned taking a call 100ft underwater.

YOU KNOW YOU'RE A MOBILE ADDICT WHEN . . .

You encourage your kids to text their lists to Father Christmas.

Don't speak to me... Just call.

YOU KNOW YOU'RE A MOBILE ADDICT WHEN . . .

You bury a mobile phone with your dearly departed...to save money on spiritual mediums.

YOU KNOW YOU'RE A MOBILE ADDICT WHEN . . .

You are banned from cinemas all over the country.

YOU KNOW YOU'RE A MOBILE ADDICT WHEN . . .

You think that World History begins with the birth of Alexander Graham Bell.

You are convinced that *ET* would have stayed on earth if he'd had a mobile.

You think you know why
the dinosaurs died out...
well, how can anything
survive without a mobile?

YOU KNOW YOU'RE A MOBILE ADDICT WHEN . . .

You write to *Jim'll Fix It* to ask if you can work in *The Link* for a day.

YOU KNOW YOU'RE A MOBILE ADDICT WHEN . . .

Your partner leaves you because you spent too much time on your (vibrating) phone.

YOU KNOW YOU'RE A MOBILE ADDICT WHEN . . .

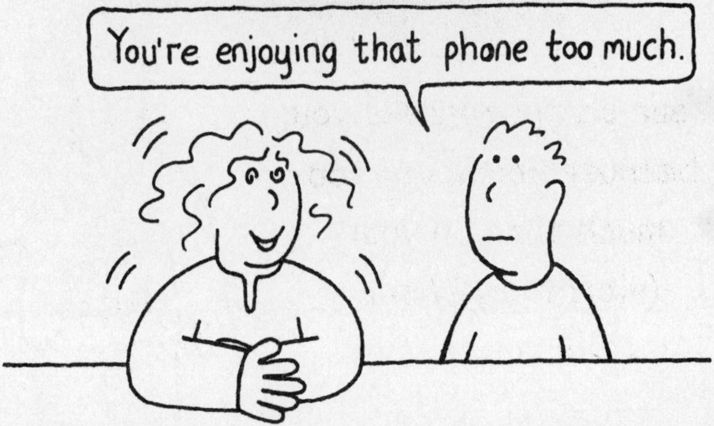

You never know what
to wear at parties but
as long as it doesn't
clash with your
mobile you're okay.

YOU KNOW YOU'RE A MOBILE ADDICT WHEN . . .

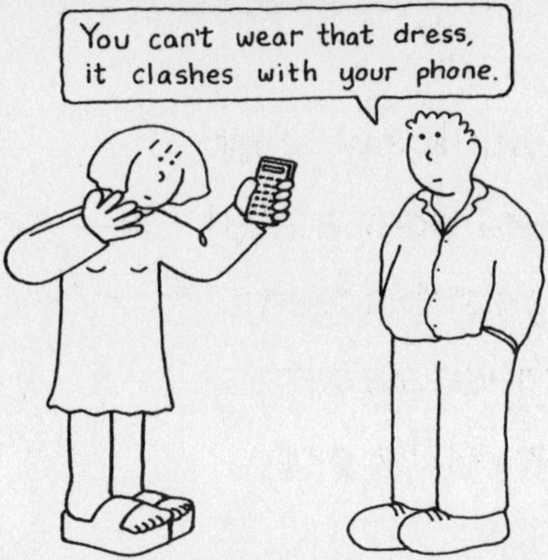

YOU KNOW YOU'RE A MOBILE ADDICT WHEN . . .

Supermarket shopping takes no time at all, because you and partner do individual aisles liaising

YOU KNOW YOU'RE A MOBILE ADDICT WHEN . . .

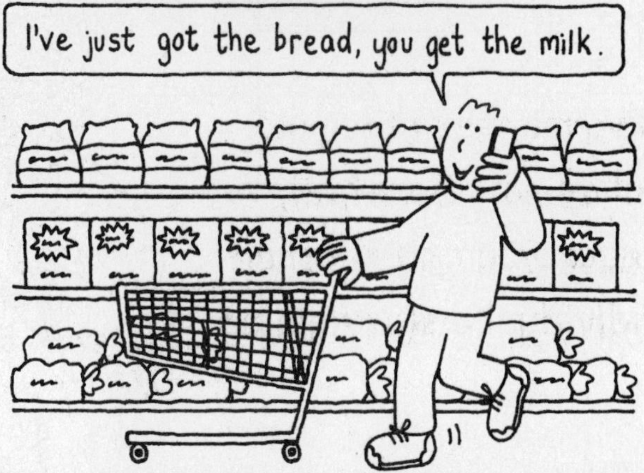

YOU KNOW YOU'RE A MOBILE ADDICT WHEN . . .

At your firstborn's christening, you refuse to let the vicar dunk your baby in the font... in case

73

YOU KNOW YOU'RE A MOBILE ADDICT WHEN . . .

You are asked to feature in a radio interview about addicts, but you miss your chance to speak... because you're on the phone.

Your car has hands-free phone sets for the passengers too... so you can speak to them whilst driving.

YOU KNOW YOU'RE A MOBILE ADDICT WHEN . . .

You treat your kids to a day out at a theme park... *Vodafone Retail Business Park* actually.

You rarely read a paper... why bother when you can get weather, traffic and sports updates via your phone (even if does take twice as long and you can only see one word at a time).

YOU KNOW YOU'RE A MOBILE ADDICT WHEN . . .

You love mobile phone technology so much you decide to emigrate to Japan...even though you hate sushi.

The only sex you've had is, not surprisingly, phone sex... and you're addicted to that too. (You really need help.)

79

Your idea of relaxation is
listening to soothing
mobile phone ring tones.

YOU KNOW YOU'RE A MOBILE ADDICT WHEN . . .

You'd text the
emergency services
rather than dial 999.

The battery runs low but
your back up is better
than the British Army's.

83

No matter what the theme, you always wear your phone outfit at fancy dress parties. You card!

YOU KNOW YOU'RE A MOBILE ADDICT WHEN . . .

Your get all dewy-eyed
and soft focused
whenever people mention
your true love –
telecommunications.

YOU KNOW YOU'RE A MOBILE ADDICT WHEN . . .

You get very touchy if anyone criticises the length of your aerial.

YOU KNOW YOU'RE A MOBILE ADDICT WHEN . . .

Your teachers at school finally gave up on you when you started text messaging your homework.

U cnt spL prprly.

YOU KNOW YOU'RE A MOBILE ADDICT WHEN . . .

You are a jealous lover...
your partner spends
more time on her
phone than yours.

Your first word was
'*Cellnet*'...and that was
when you were 20.

91

You commission a portrait of your favourite phone.

YOU KNOW YOU'RE A
MOBILE ADDICT WHEN . . .

Even your wife thinks your mobile obsession has gone too far and calls for an injunction to be taken out against your phone.

YOU KNOW YOU'RE A MOBILE ADDICT WHEN . . .

You dream in LCD.

Your hottest fantasy
features you naked with
the next generation of
mobile phones.

You have 'his and its'
matching towel and
dressing gown sets made
for you and your *Ericsson*.

You hold your wedding list at *World of Phones.*

Even your baby photos
feature you clasping a
dummy to your ear.

Most kids have an imaginary friend. You had one too... but you only communicated via your imaginary phone. Sweet.

You insist that more mobile phone masts are erected in the Alps when you take your annual skiing trip...you simply can't risk missing a call whilst on piste.

You are so used to
having a headache that,
on the rare occasions that
you don't, you call your
GP in a panic... and give
her one instead.

YOU KNOW YOU'RE A MOBILE ADDICT WHEN . . .

You glow brighter than the *ReadyBrek* kid.

YOU KNOW YOU'RE A MOBILE ADDICT WHEN . . .

You are so proud of your new twins...a couple of ickle *Motorola StarTac*s.

YOU KNOW YOU'RE A MOBILE ADDICT WHEN . . .

You have to hide your phone bills from the wife...underneath your stash of dirty mags.

You've just had your baby's nursery redecorated, complete with a new cradle... a phone cradle, that is.

YOU KNOW YOU'RE A MOBILE ADDICT WHEN . . .

You swap the furry dice in your car for a pair of furry mobiles.

YOU KNOW YOU'RE A MOBILE ADDICT WHEN . . .

You lost your mobile...and all record of your friends. Actually, your list of stored numbers was the only known proof that you had any mates at all.

Don't speak to me... Just call.

YOU KNOW YOU'RE A
MOBILE ADDICT WHEN . . .

You sleep with
your head-set on.

You learnt a piece from your *one2one* instruction manual for an audition with the RSC... and they were very impressed with the passion in your speech.

110

YOU KNOW YOU'RE A MOBILE ADDICT WHEN . . .

You've made yourself double-jointed... so you can hold a mobile with your foot in case you ever break both arms.

YOU KNOW YOU'RE A MOBILE ADDICT WHEN . . .

You break your spine and
suggest that the surgeons
replace it with a mobile
phone mast instead.

Your will states that all money be left to telecommunications research... if there's any left once your mobile-shaped mausoleum is completed.

A mobile phone showed up on your own 5-month scan... but your worried mother felt it was too late to have you aborted.

YOU KNOW YOU'RE A MOBILE ADDICT WHEN . . .

You are the first person
to develop RSI of the ear.

You think *Nokia* is a really
pretty name for a girl...
your daughter's not
so sure.

117

YOU KNOW YOU'RE A MOBILE ADDICT WHEN . . .

You do your bit for charity by pledging money to Comic Relief... on the proviso that your hefty donation is spent on improving 3rd World telecommunications (by bringing the convenience of dial-a-pizza to famine-afflicted areas).

Don't speak to me... Just call.

You commission an award-
winning architect to
design a library for all
your interesting phone-
related literature and
instruction manuals.

YOU KNOW YOU'RE A
MOBILE ADDICT WHEN . . .

Your philosophy on life
is 'pay as you go'.

YOU KNOW YOU'RE A MOBILE ADDICT WHEN . . .

You don't worry when your kids are born deaf... they'll learn how to text in no time.

YOU KNOW YOU'RE A MOBILE ADDICT WHEN . . .

Your head is more radioactive than Sellafield, which is handy... you can cook a chicken in under 3 minutes just by breathing on it.

You are even asked to
leave Mobile Addicts
Anonymous because you
suggest that the 12 steps
could be conducted over
the phone.

123

YOU KNOW YOU'RE A MOBILE ADDICT WHEN . . .

You're so obsessed, you
even buy jokes about
mobile phones!

**For the latest humour books
from Summersdale, check out**